The Life Insurance Handbook

Louis S. Shuntich J.D., LL.M.

MARKETPLACE BOOKS
COLUMBIA, MARYLAND

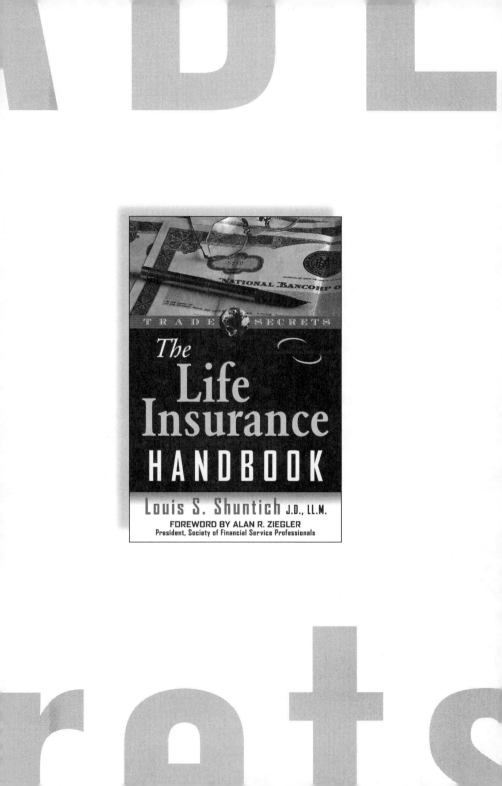

TRADE SECRETS

The
Life
Insurance
HANDBOOK

Louis S. Shuntich J.D., LL.M.

FOREWORD BY ALAN R. ZIEGLER
President, Society of Financial Service Professionals

This book, along with other books, is available at discounts that make it realistic to provide them as gifts to your customers, clients, and staff. For more information on these long lasting, cost effective premiums, please call John Boyer at 800.272.2855 or you may email him at john@fpbooks.com

ISBN 1-59280-057-2

Printed in the United States of America.

This book is dedicated to my daughter Savanna.

Contents

Chapter 4:

How to Evaluate and Compare
Life Insurance Companies

Chapter 5:

The Federal Tax Treatment of Life Insurance

Chapter 6:

Traps and Pitfalls to be Avoided

Glossary

Resource Guide

Foreword

Dear Financial Service Professional:

Term life insurance. Whole life. Variable, Universal and First-to-die Life. The sheer number of distinct products available - as well as the many manufacturers and the widely different uses and tax implications of each make advising a customer in connection with a life insurance policy a fairly complicated feat. Couple that with a constantly changing industry - and a financial professional may understandably feel overwhelmed by the sheer volume of choices and information.

The Society of Financial Service Professionals, has teamed up with tax and estate planning expert Louis S. Shuntich, Esq., and the publishing arm of FP Books to bring you a practical new reference guide to the industry that is both compact and comprehensive. It addresses the various tax issues that must be evaluated, and provides comparison criteria needed to draw sound conclusions. In short - it's a great learning tool for keeping busy financial professionals up to date on this wide-ranging topic.

Since its inception, The Society of Financial Service Professionals has been dedicated to providing lifelong learning to its membership. While our industry, our culture, our society have changed significantly over the past 75 years, our dedication to ongoing education has never wavered.

The Society distinguishes itself among other financial service membership organizations with its requirement that members hold a recognized degree or credential, such as CLU, CFP, CPA, JD, ChFC, or CEBS. The Society's goal is to create an inclusive professional home for these credentialed individuals who share a belief in a core set of values - education, ethics, and relationships.

As the professional home for our members, the Society promotes an environment of professional growth and development and provides the tools to support such growth through our Code of Professional

Responsibility, access to networking opportunities, and continuing education programs and services.

A steadfast commitment to continuing education that is current, comprehensive, and practical is a cornerstone of the Society's mission statement. We are proud to further this mission by bringing you *The Life Insurance Handbook.* We trust you will find it an informative, interesting, and useful aide in your professional learning and development - and look forward to carrying on the tradition of quality education through our continuing education courses, seminars, periodicals and new books.

Good luck - and happy travels - on your journey of professional development.

Alan R. Ziegler, CEBS, CLU, ChFC
President, Society of Financial Service Professionals

Introduction

Any consideration of the purchase of life insurance begins with an understanding that the policy pays a benefit upon the death of the insured, whether that event happens on the day the contract is issued or fifty years later. This totally unique feature is unmatched by any other financial instrument and makes life insurance suitable for family, business and charitable purposes, where a relatively large amount of funds will be needed but there is no certainty that adequate time will be available for their accumulation. Further, cash values that grow on a tax-deferred basis, are available for a variety of personal and business objectives as diverse as paying a child's college tuition or funding an employee's supplemental retirement income.

The sheer number of manufacturers, variety of products and differences between policies of the same type, however, make giving advice in connection with the purchase of life insurance a daunting task. Yet, as with any other venture, doing one's homework can make a great difference in the outcome.

To that end, the purpose of this book is to facilitate the process by succinctly providing information on certain legal aspects to acquiring and owning a policy, the types of contracts that are available, the means for evaluating and comparing policies and insurance companies and the tax treatment of life insurance products.

Finally, due to the complexity of the law and the transactions in which life insurance is used, advice is provided on how to recognize and avoid traps and pitfalls that might be incurred.

The
Life Insurance
Handbook

Louis S. Shuntich J.D., LL.M.

Chapter 1

The Life Insurance Policy

The process of acquiring a life insurance policy requires meeting certain conditions imposed by the law and the issuing insurance company. Further, while policies are approved by state insurance departments, in accordance with laws and regulations that are intended to protect consumers, they are complicated and contain many variations. The following is a summary of some of the pertinent laws and policy provisions with which a prospective policyholder should be familiar before beginning the process of acquiring coverage.

Insurable interest. The acquisition of a policy starts with determining that the prospective purchaser has an insurable interest in the life to be insured. That is because, without an insurable interest, the policy would be unenforceable under the law. This is based on public policy considerations that are designed to prevent people from being insured for no purpose other than their being killed for the death proceeds.

An insurable interest is found to exist where the prospective purchaser can reasonably expect to receive financial gain from the proposed insured's longevity or can expect to suffer financial loss from his death. In that regard, a prospective insured is deemed to have an insurable interest, for an unlimited amount, in his own life with the right to name anyone he chooses as beneficiary. Insurance companies, however, limit the amount of coverage they will issue to a figure that is not unreasonably large, relative to the insured's financial situation and earning capacity.

Relationships based on marriage and close blood ties that presumably involve pecuniary interests also serve as a basis for finding an insurable interest. This is also true of debtor creditor relationships, with the understanding that the amount of coverage must bear some reasonable relationship to the amount of debt. In addition, many other business relationships provide a basis for insurable interest as long as there is a substantial economic tie between the parties such as between an employer and an employee or the partners of a partnership.

Generally, an insurable interest only needs to exist when the contract is issued unless state law or the policy provides otherwise. This means that the contract will continue to be valid and enforceable even if the insurable interest later ceases. An exception to this rule exists in those states that also require an insurable interest between the insured and the beneficiary, where the interest must go on.

Policy application. Acquiring a life insurance policy begins with completing a policy application. That document, which generally becomes a part of the contract, requires that the proposed insured accurately provide information on his medical, personal and family history as well as employment and lifestyle. Information on other life insurance in force or applied for is also required.

Depending upon the law of the governing jurisdiction, the contract may be void or voidable by the insurer if the applicant does not accurately disclose all material information called for. In that regard, a fact may be considered material if its disclosure would have affected the insurer's willingness to issue the policy under the same terms or for the same premium. The applicant's intentions may also be relevant but the courts tend to liberally interpret situations in favor of the applicant.

Incontestable clause. This is a clause in life insurance contracts that prevents the insurer from voiding the contract on grounds of concealment, material misrepresentation or fraud after a certain period of time (usually two years). If the insured lives or dies within the contestable period, the insurer can contest the contract but not thereafter. The purpose of this provision is to give finality to an arrangement upon which the beneficiaries depend and which becomes increasingly difficult for them to defend with the passage of time.

Suicide clause. This provision typically states that the insurance company will terminate the contract and return the premiums if the insured commits suicide within one or two years of the original application date. In such cases the burden of proof is with the insurer and it usually represents a difficult challenge.

Contract interpretation. The courts' general leaning in favor of policy owners extends to interpreting policy provisions. Further, some jurisdictions even give effect to the policyholders' reasonable expectations, where they conflict with the policies' explicit

> Life insurance policies are written by the life insurance companies, without the bargaining or input from purchasers that characterizes most contract relationships.

terms. All this seems to be a reflection of the fact that life insurance policies are written by the life insurance companies, without the bargaining or input from purchasers that characterizes most contract relationships.

Jurisdiction. Contracts are generally governed by the laws of the jurisdictions in which they are made, as evidenced by the locations of the parties, their relationships and actions within the jurisdiction in question. In that regard, when it comes to life insurance, state laws, courts and insurance departments do not take lightly jurisdictional issues with regard to those domiciled within their borders. This means that for a particular state's law to apply to an insurance policy, the parties should have significant contact with that jurisdiction through domicile, employment or business activities. Consequently, merely crossing borders with the intention of executing an application for a policy within a jurisdiction for the sole purpose of gaining some advantage under that state's law is likely to lead to disappointment.

Effective date of insurance. Applications may be submitted with or without payment of the first premium. If the application is sent in without a premium, it is considered to be an invitation for the insurer to make an offer to contract by issuing the policy. The applicant may then accept the offer and put the coverage in effect by accepting the policy upon delivery and paying the requisite premium.

Alternatively, if the applicant submits the first premium with the application, some form of receipt may or may not be given in return. If no receipt is given, the policy will not take effect until it is issued and delivered to the policy owner. More often, however, a receipt is given and results in some form of temporary insurance, for a limited amount, until the actual policy is delivered.

Grace period. This policy provision requires the insurance company to accept premiums for a certain period after they are due, without requiring evidence of insurability. The contract remains in effect during the grace period, which is typically from 31 to 61 days, depending on the type of contract. The purpose of the provision is to protect the policy owner from the consequences of an unintentional lapse of the policy. The insurer is also protected, however, to the extent that it is permitted to deduct the premium plus interest from any death proceeds, if the insured dies during the grace period.

The grace period protects the policy owner from the consequences of an unintentional lapse of the policy.

Reinstatement clause. This type of provision gives the policyholder the right to reinstate a policy after it has lapsed, for a certain period, if he meets certain requirements. Generally, this means that he has to provide evidence of insurability and pay the overdue premiums.

Nonforfeiture provision. This kind of provision only applies to cash value policies and gives the policyholder, who chooses to terminate his contract, the options of applying the cash surrender value to:

- Give the policyholder cash.
- Provide a reduced paid-up policy of the same type.
- Provide extended term insurance for the original face amount.

Chapter 2

The Types and Features of Life Insurance Policies

Term life insurance. A term policy pays a death benefit if the insured dies within the specified time period or term of coverage stated in the contract. If the insured survives the term, the policy expires without any value since such contracts generally have no cash value or dividends. A term policy's lack of cash value and limited period of coverage results in premiums that are initially lower than those of cash value insurance. The price to pay, however, is that a term policy's premiums dramatically increase as the insured grows older. In addition, term policies usually provide a level death benefit, but term with a gradually decreasing death benefit (decreasing term) is also common and a way of keeping premiums level as the insured ages. Further, a term policyholder has the right, under certain policies, to renew the coverage for additional "terms" or convert it to (exchange it for) a cash value policy without evidence of insurability.

• **Renewable term.** Term policies may provide coverage for a period as short as one year but usually provide protection for a set number of years or to a stated age. In addition, as previously stated, term policies may be renewable. This means that the policyholder has the contractual right to

> **The right to continue the coverage at a predetermined price can be an extremely valuable right.**

extend the coverage for successive terms without evidence of insurability. The premiums are level for a specific duration of coverage but increase with each renewal to reflect the insured's increased age. Finally, the right to renew is generally limited to a specified age such as 65 or 70. It should be noted that if the policy is not renewable, the policyholder has no right to continue the coverage and must apply for a new policy with evidence of insurability. In that regard, as an individual ages, the chances that he will remain insurable or be able to obtain coverage at a price he is willing and able to pay decreases. Consequently, the right to continue the coverage at a predetermined price can be an extremely valuable right.

• **Convertible term.** Term insurance can be convertible, which means that the policyholder can exchange the term coverage for a cash value policy without evidence of insurability. This adds a great deal of flexibility to an individual's overall insurance plan. That is because an individual who has a permanent need for coverage but who cannot afford cash value insurance can start with a term policy and convert it to a cash value (permanent) policy when his financial situation improves. Further, convertibility is a way of protecting against the loss of insurability as the covered individual ages. As previously noted, a renewal provision provides similar protection but the limit on the age at which most such policies can be renewed makes having coverage when needed less certain than occurs with a conversion feature. Caution should be exercised, however, in that the right to convert is often shorter than the maximum duration of the policy.

- **Level and non-level face amount policies.** As previously stated, most term policies have a level death benefit over the period of the policy. On the other hand, there is a substantial market for decreasing term insurance. This is because such coverage can avoid the problem of increasing premiums and can be used to cover a declining need for protection, as occurs with so called "mortgage" insurance or business loans. Typically, such policies are not renewable but are issued for durations as long as 30 years.

- **Suitable uses for term insurance.** Term insurance is most useful under the following circumstances:

    1. The need for insurance coverage is known to be temporary. This may occur with a family having a home mortgage, young children or those approaching financial independence. In addition, from a business perspective it might be used to cover business debts or to provide key employee protection during the employee's working years.

    2. Cash value coverage is preferable but the prospective policyholder lacks sufficient cash flow to cover such premiums or cannot afford them. In such cases, a renewable and convertible term policy would be more affordable and would provide the option to acquire more permanent protection at the appropriate time.

    3. There is a need to supplement cash value coverage. This can be done with various term riders that can be attached to a cash value policy. Much flexibility and specific tailoring to the insurance needs and financial resources of a policyholder can be accomplished in this manner.

4. Buy term and invest the difference. This approach is suggested for those individuals who need and can afford cash value protection but prefer to invest the initial difference between term and cash value premiums in an investment vehicle that is expected to outperform a cash value policy. This concept is valid for those individuals who have the discipline to regularly invest the difference in premiums and have the business acumen to outperform the cash value policy. Such individuals are not common and the desire for higher returns and more investment control might be accomplished through the acquisition of a variable life insurance policy as later described in this chapter.

Cash value life insurance. These types of policies that are sometimes referred to as "permanent" or "whole life" insurance typically require level premiums over the duration of the contract, which runs from the date of issue until the insured's death. In the early years of the policy the premiums exceed the contract's mortality costs. These excess premiums and earnings thereon generate cash values that are used in later years to offset the higher mortality cost as the insured gets older and allow for the policy to have level premiums.

> **Cash value life insurance, sometimes referred to as "permanent" or "whole life" insurance, typically requires level premiums over the duration of the contract.**

The cash values are generally lower in the early years because of sales and issue charges but they increase at a somewhat constant rate until they reach the policy's face amount at around age 100. In addition, the cash values are available to the policy owner at any time through policy loans or surrenders. In that respect, such policies contain schedules of minimum guaranteed cash values that are available to the policy owner at selected points in time.

The premiums paid to the insurance company are held in the company's general account and the company decides in which assets such funds are invested. In addition, many cash value policies are "participating" contracts, which means that the company passes on to the policy owner its favorable mortality, investment and expense experience through policy dividends. Those dividends may be taken as cash, used to reduce premiums, left at interest or used to purchase PUAs. Conversely, a cash value policy may be non-participating, which means that the policy owner will not participate in the company's favorable experience.

• **Suitable uses for cash value insurance.** Cash value policies are generally best, with respect to cost, for those with insurance needs of a long duration since the front-end charges negatively affect policy values in the early years. In any case, where the insurance need is long term or permanent and there is a desire to maintain a fixed premium cost, such coverage may be appropriate for the following specific purposes among others:

- Long-term financial security for a family in respect to replacing lost earnings from the premature death of a parent.
- Certainty that funds will be available for a child's college education through death benefits or access to cash values.
- Liquidity for estate settlement needs such as last expenses and death taxes.

- Funding for business buy & sell agreements.

- Key person insurance.

- Funding for charitable bequests.

• **Limited-payment cash value insurance.** This variation of cash value insurance provides coverage for the insured's whole life but the premiums are payable for a limited period after which the policy becomes paid-up. It is most useful where the policy owner can afford the higher premiums to pay-up the coverage and does not want long-term premium requirements because of approaching retirement or involvement in a career with limited earning years, such as occurs in sports. It is also useful for business purposes where the desire is to fund obligations over fixed periods such as to provide deferred compensation benefits.

> In the redetermination period, the company may recalculate the premiums and possibly the face amount.

Current-assumption whole life insurance. This type of product, that is sometimes referred to as "interest sensitive whole life", is like cash value life insurance in that at the time of issue the premium and death benefit levels are fixed. Those amounts may change, however, after a time called the "redetermination period" at which point the company may recalculate the premium and possibly the face amount using new assumptions as to future interest earnings and mortality charges.

In addition, these policies are "unbundled" in that specific allocations are made of premiums and interest earnings to policy expenses, mortality charges and cash values through an accumulation account. This practice is intended to give the policyholder a better picture of how the contract functions in terms of the allocation of premiums and earnings. Note, however, that while such contracts contain certain minimum interest and maximum mortality guarantees, the actual charges to the accumulation account are based on current experience. This means that the balance of the accumulation account in future years is uncertain, and adjustments may be required to future premiums at the end of a redetermination period to maintain a certain level of death benefit.

• **Suitable uses for current assumption whole life.** This type of policy is useful where the policyholder wants the potential for better investment results than are usually associated with regular cash value insurance. The problem, however, is that while such contracts contain a minimum guaranteed cash value, premiums may have to be increased or the face amount decreased if the policy's performance does not meet expectations.

Adjustable life insurance. This type of cash value insurance allows the policyholder to reconfigure the contract, within limits, to another form of term or whole life policy. Specifically, the policyholder may increase or decrease the premium, face amount, protection period and/or premium payment period. Some limitations on this flexibility are that increases in face amount usually require evidence of insurability and a minimum annual premium is required to keep the policy in force. In addition, changes are prospective and usually only permitted at specified intervals upon notice to the insurer. Further, between such intervals the policy has a level premium and death benefit with a set cash value schedule that does not generally permit withdrawals without a complete or partial surrender of the policy.

• **Suitable uses for adjustable life.** These types of policies are recommended where the policy owner seeks greater flexibility than is usually associated with regular cash value insurance. In that respect, the ability to reconfigure the contract allows the policyholder to respond to future changes in circumstances. This feature makes the product attractive to both the personal and business markets.

Variable life insurance. This product was first offered in the mid 1970s and is a cash value type of policy under which the policyholder may direct the investment of cash values among a variety of investment options that are similar to mutual funds. In that regard, it is a fixed premium whole life product that, because of its investment features, offers a variable death benefit that is tied to investment results. This reflects the objective of creating a product whose underlying cash values would be invested in equities for the purpose of keeping the policyholders' insurance protection in pace with inflation.

> With variable life insurance, the policyholder may direct the investment of cash values among a variety of investment options.

This is accomplished by investing premiums less insurance charges in an account that is separate from the insurer's general account that backs traditional insurance products. The separate account acts as a mutual fund in which the policyholder selects, within limits, how his premiums are to be allocated among various sub-accounts. These sub-accounts offer a variety of investment choices that range from conservative to aggressively managed funds. As result of the investment experience of the selected sub-accounts, the policy's cash values and death benefits can increase or decrease at the risk of the policy owner. The contract, however, carries a guarantee that the death benefit will not fall below a certain minimum and some policies even provide a guaranteed minimum return.

The death benefit is made up of the minimum death benefit guaranteed plus additional units of variable insurance that are purchased on a regular basis with earnings that exceed an assumed rate of return. Conversely, if the investment results are lower than the assumed rate of return, previously purchased variable insurance units are surrendered and the total death benefit is reduced.

• **Suitable uses of variable life.** This product is suitable for parties seeking a cash value fixed level premium product that offers investment choices with the potential for equity type performance that may keep pace with inflation. It must be noted, however, that the product places the risk of unfavorable investment results directly on the policyholder.

Universal life insurance. This product was introduced in 1979 and built on prior developments by offering a combination of flexible premiums, current assumptions, adjustable death benefits and an unbundling of the savings and insurance elements of the contract. This means that after paying the initial premium the policyholder can modify at any time the amount, date and frequency of premium payments as well as the amount of the death benefit. In effect, as long as there is sufficient cash value to pay the necessary insurance charges, the contract can range from term coverage to a paid-up policy.

To overcome the ease with which a policyholder might allow his contract to lapse because of the absence of required premium payments, companies bill for a planned or target premium that is set within suggested limits by the policy owner. Further, some companies guarantee that a policy will not lapse, even though the cash value is exhausted, provided that the policyholder maintains a specified minimum premium payment in all years.

To assist policyholders in determining how to best utilize their contracts' flexibility, universal life contracts are illustrated in an unbundled format. In that respect, each year's illustrations show how the loads and mortality costs are charged against a cash account that is also credited with the current interest rate. Essentially, the policy's cash value is determined by taking the prior period's balance and adding to it premium payments, plus current interest earnings, and deducting from it expenses and mortality charges. The result is that, with the above information at the end of each period, the policyholder is in an informed position to modify his coverage and premium input to meet his changing needs.

It should be noted that universal life policies guarantee that a minimum rate of interest will be credited to cash values. In addition, such values are available to the policyholder through policy loans and partial surrenders.

Universal life policies usually provide two death benefit options. They are Option A, under which the death benefit is fixed and as the cash value increases the amount at risk automatically decreases. Alternatively, Option B provides a specified death benefit plus the policy's cash value. (This means that as the cash value increases the total death benefit automatically increases.) Such flexibility does not come, however, without cost. These contracts are generally more expensive for insurance companies to administer. These costs are reflected in the charges against the cash account. A few companies offer an Option C which provides in addition to the selected death benefit, an additional death benefit equal to all premiums paid. This option is particularly appropriate in business cases using a split dollar plan. As with other options, there is an attendant cost resulting in additional charges to the cash account.

• **Suitable uses for universal life.** The extraordinary flexibility of universal life results in its being marketed as the only policy a person will ever need. This is because of the policy owner's ability to reconfigure the contract by changing premiums and/or death benefits to meet different circumstances. Consequently, it is popular in the family market for young couples with children who can concentrate on death benefits in the early years, cash values for college years and retirement and finally death benefits for estate liquidity.

> Universal life insurance is being marketed as the only policy a person will ever need because of its extraordinary flexibilty.

Similarly, universal life's flexibility makes it popular in the business market as well. This is because it is a good vehicle for funding business needs such as buy & sell agreements and employee benefits such as deferred compensation and split dollar.

Variable universal life insurance. This type of product combines the separate account/sub-account investment features of variable life with the premium payment and death benefit flexibility of universal life. The policy owner bears the investment risk associated with the assets supporting the policy's cash values since those values are determined as a pro rata share of the assets in the respective sub-accounts selected by the policy owner.

Death benefits are determined in accordance with the Option A and Option B type offerings of a universal life policy. Accordingly, under Option A the death benefit is fixed and as the cash value increases the amount at risk automatically decreases. Alternatively, Option B provides a specified death benefit plus the policy's cash value. (This means that as cash values increase the death benefit automatically increases.)

• **Suitable uses for variable universal life.** This type of product is suitable for those parties who want the premium and death benefit flexibility of universal life with the investment orientation of variable life. In that regard, they should possess the financial discipline and investment acumen to deal with the responsibility as well as resources to bear the risk of adverse investment performance.

First-to-die life insurance. This type of policy covers the lives of two or more people jointly and pays a death benefit on the death of the first-to-die. The premium is less than would be paid on separate individual cash value policies covering the same lives. The problem, however, is that after the first death there is no coverage on the remaining lives. This is somewhat mitigated by the fact that such policies usually allow the survivors to acquire individual cash value policies on their lives without having to provide evidence of insurability.

> **The problem with first-to-die insurance is that after the first death there is no coverage on the remaining lives**

• **Suitable uses for first-to-die insurance.** This kind of insurance is typically used to provide financial protection for married couples and to fund business buy & sell arrangements.

Second-to-die (survivorship) life insurance. This type of policy that is sometimes called survivorship insurance covers two or more lives and pays a death benefit upon the death of the last to die. It can take the form of term, whole life or universal life insurance. In addition, such contracts may contain a provision that permits the policy to be split into separate policies

> **Second-to-die insurance is particulaly useful for married children.**

for each insured on certain events, such as the divorce of an insured married couple or the repeal of the estate tax law.

• **Suitable uses for second-to-die insurance.** Most often this type of insurance covers a husband and wife. This reflects the fact that it was designed primarily to provide liquidity for federal estate taxes where the couple postpones all such taxes until the second death through the use of the unlimited marital deduction. Further, since no benefit is paid until the second death, this type of coverage is generally less costly than the combined cost of separate policies.

This coverage is also particularly useful for married couples with children since the greatest threat to the children's security comes from the loss of both parents.

Optional policy provisions and riders. Once a particular type of policy is identified as being most suitable to a prospective purchaser's needs, additional tailoring can be accomplished to better fit the policy to the purchaser's particular situation through the use of optional policy provisions and riders. A description of those optional features is as follows:

- **Waiver of premium.** This type of provision relieves the policy owner from the obligation to pay premiums or other charges required to keep a policy in force if he becomes totally and permanently disabled before a particular age.

- **Disability income rider.** This benefit provides a monthly income payment to the policy owner upon his total and permanent disability from illness or injury after a certain waiting period.

- **Accidental death benefit.** These types of riders or policy clauses provide that a multiple of the face amount will be paid if the insured dies because of an accident.

- **Cost of living rider.** This feature permits a policyholder's coverage to be increased to keep pace with inflation.

- **Term riders.** These are term coverages that may be added to a basic cash value policy to increase the amount of insurance in a more affordable way.

- **Option to purchase additional insurance.** This feature permits a policy owner to purchase additional amounts of coverage at specific intervals without having to provide evidence of insurability. It is a way for an individual to guarantee his insurability.

- **Accelerated death benefit.** These policy provisions or riders provide for the payment of all or part of the policy's death benefits prior to the insured's death under certain circumstances, where evidence of terminal illness is shown.

Chapter 3

How to Evaluate and Compare Life Insurance Policies

Evaluating a policy. The most commonly used tool for evaluating a life insurance policy is the policy's illustration. A life insurance policy illustration is prepared by an insurer to demonstrate how a policy is structured and how it may perform over an insured's lifetime using a set of projections that include both guaranteed and non-guaranteed elements. As to the non-guaranteed elements, it is critical to understand that the projections reflect a set of assumptions as to the insurer's mortality experience, investment returns, loading charges and lapse rates. The key to an illustration's credibility, therefore, is the reasonableness of those underlying assumptions, and the best indication of their reasonableness is the insurer's past performance. Information on an insurer's performance may be obtained from a company agent, the state insurance department, the NAIC and the SEC. In addition, The Society of Financial Service Professionals provides illustration questionnaires for variable and non-variable products to insurers that are completed on a voluntary basis. The questions are designed to determine whether the insurers' illustrations are predicated on realistic figures and to gain an indication of how much actual policy values may vary. This information is available to agents and other professional advisors for the benefit of prospective purchasers. Finally, the A.M. Best Company provides Bests' Key Rating Guide, which gives five-year financial summaries of insurance companies.

Comparing policies. One approach to comparing policies utilizes various mathematical cost comparison methods. The problem with this approach is that it is likely to only be attractive to the mathematically inclined. Further, such methods rely upon illustrated policy values that may vary greatly from actual values for a particular company. Moreover, the underlying basis for one company's illustration may be different from the next, so that it is difficult to compare apples to apples even when the same type of policy is involved.

> Rather then searching for the cheapest coverage, find a policy suitable to the policyholder's needs and issued by a company likely to provide good service.

Another way of obtaining and comparing the costs of similar policies is to use the "Interest Adjusted Net Cost" (IANC) indexes (net payment cost index and surrender cost index) that are required by the NAIC Life Insurance Model Regulation and regularly provided by many insurers in their illustrations. These figures take into account the time value of money and give the cost per $1,000 of death benefits (guaranteed & non-guaranteed) and cash values.

When using illustrations for comparison purposes, always make sure that the agent provides all the pages and not just a summary or select number of pages. In addition, ask for projections using different interest rates that reflect what might realistically be expected to happen over the long term and, in setting such rates, consider the prospective policyholder's tolerance for risk. Remember also that comparisons based on illustrated figures are only as credible as the companies that prepare them. Further, a numerical comparison of policies has a deceiving quality of precision that does not exist in the real world. Consequently, rather than just searching for what appears to be the cheapest coverage, the analysis should focus on finding a policy that is suitable for the policyholder's needs and is issued by a company that is most likely to provide good service and be around to fulfill its guaranteed promises and reasonable projections. In that regard, valuable assistance may be obtained from an experienced agent with appropriate credentials, such as a CLU (Chartered Life Underwriter), and suitable references.

Chapter 4

How to Evaluate and Compare Life Insurance Companies

Evaluating an insurance company. An evaluation of any insurance company begins with an analysis of its financial stability because of the long-term nature of its obligation to the policyholder. The most critical factor in making this determination is the adequacy of its surplus. For this purpose the term "surplus" is defined as the excess of the insurer's assets over its liabilities. In judging the validity of the surplus figure, however, it is necessary to look to the quality of the assets the insurer holds. This is because of the varying degrees of risk that are associated with different classes of assets and between assets of the same class. (For example corporate "junk bonds" cannot compare in degree of risk with bonds issued by the U.S Treasury.) Further, the profitability of a company is crucial to its ability to meet future obligations.

Comparing companies. Sources of information for making the above evaluations and then comparing companies are similar to those previously mentioned for determining an insurer's past performance, i.e., the government and trade associations. The effective gathering, assimilation and accurate interpretation of such information is, however, a task more often better left to specialists such as the five rating agencies that focus on insurers (Standard & Poor, Duff & Phelps, A. M. Best, Moody and Weiss). Each agency has a schedule of ratings that are kept current and readily provide an idea of an insurer's financial standing. The ratings from one agency to another are not perfectly comparable, however, since each has its own grading system using alphabetical letters and not all insurers are graded by all five agencies. Further, the subjective nature of the evaluation process results in insurers receiving different valuations from the various agencies. In any case, the ratings are a reasonably reliable, valuable and a convenient source of information on a complex subject that should not be overlooked. Generally, information on a company's ratings and related reports can be obtained from the insurer's agents and customer service operations as well as the rating agencies' own web sites on the Internet.

> **The most critical factor in determining financial stability is the adequacy of an insurance company's surplus.**

Chapter 5

The Federal Tax Treatment of Life Insurance

Federal income tax treatment. Life insurance proceeds were excluded from income when the federal income tax was adopted in 1913. By the late 1970's and early 1980's, however, sales presentations evolved to demonstrate how the tax deferred treatment of cash values could be combined with high interest rates to generate dramatic results. This emphasis on the investment potential of life insurance caused Congress to reassess the appropriateness of the tax benefits of a product that was changing in character from insurance protection to an investment vehicle. As a result, Congress passed the Tax Equity and Fiscal Responsibility Act of 1982 or "TEFRA", which created new Internal Revenue Code subsection 101(f). This subsection was of a temporary nature and focused only on flexible premium products. Its objective was to limit investment opportunities by adopting a definition of life insurance that imposed maximum premium and minimum risk requirements on such policies.

Subsequently, Congress enacted IRC Section 7702 as a part of the Deficit Reduction Act of 1984. That provision set forth a definition of life insurance that is generally applicable to policies issued after 1984. It restricts the favorable income tax treatment of life insurance to contracts that meet tests limiting the amount of cash values or premiums that are allowed in respect to certain benefits provided under a policy. These tests require complex actuarial computations that are designed to limit favorable income tax treatment to policies that are not overly investment oriented. Specifically, to be treated as a life insurance contract under Section 7702, a policy must meet applicable state law requirements and qualify under either of the two following alternative tests:

> **During a contract's first 15 years, cash values "forced out" under the rules of IRC section 7702, because of a reduction in death benefits, are fully or partially taxable to the extent of gain in the contract.**

• **Cash value accumulation test.** The cash surrender value of the policy cannot at any time exceed the net single premium that would have to be paid at such time to fund future benefits under the policy.

• **Guideline premium and cash value corridor test.** This test has two components, both of which must be met, in order for the policy to qualify as life insurance. They are as follows:

- **Guideline premium.** To meet this requirement, the sum of the premiums paid under the policy cannot at any time exceed the greater of the "guideline single premium" (the amount required to fund certain future benefits under the policy) or the "sum of the guideline level premiums" (the level annual amount that is payable over a period not ending before the insured is 95 and necessary to fund certain future benefits under the policy) to that date.

- **Cash value corridor.** The death benefit under the policy at any time is equal to or greater than the applicable percentage of the cash surrender value. These percentages are set forth in a table under IRC 7702(d)(2). It should be noted that during a contract's first 15 years, cash values that are "forced out" under the rules of IRC Section 7702, because of a reduction in death benefits, are fully or partially taxable to the extent of gain in the contract. The taxable amount depends upon when the force out occurs, with payments during the first five years subject to a higher degree of taxation than payments during the rest of the 15 year period.

Consequences of failure to qualify as life insurance under IRC 7702. The above tests place a substantial burden on life insurance companies to make certain that their contracts are treated as life insurance for tax purposes. If a policy fails to qualify, it will be treated as a combination of term insurance and a currently taxable deposit fund. The result is that income must be recognized on the policy annually. The amount of income is calculated by deducting from that year's net increase in the surrender value the sum of the year's premium and deemed cost of insurance. (The amount of income is subject to withholding and reporting by the insurer.) Further, the failure to qualify will cause the portion of the policy's death proceeds equal to the cash value to lose income tax free status under IRC 101(a)(1). The balance of the death proceeds however, will be received income tax free by the beneficiary.

Premiums. The payment of premiums by an individual is considered to be a nondeductible personal expense for federal income tax purposes. Premiums paid on a policy owned by a charity are, however, deductible as a charitable contribution. Also, premium payments by an employer for an employee's life insurance protection are generally deductible by the employer as a business expense and taxable to the employee as income.

Dividends. The payment of dividends by an insurer is generally considered to be a nontaxable return of premiums regardless of the dividend option chosen by the policy owner. (Note that if dividends are left to accumulate, the interest earned will be taxable.) An exception exists where the dividends received exceed the premiums paid. In such cases, the amount of dividends in excess of total premiums paid constitutes ordinary income. Another exception applies when the policy fails to meet the definition of life insurance or is a Modified Endowment Contract or "MEC" (to be explained below). In such cases, the dividends are taxable as ordinary income unless they are applied to purchase paid-up additional insurance or "PUAs".

> **Upon the surrender of a policy, the cost basis of the policy is deducted from the gross amount received to determine the taxable income.**

Cash surrenders. The cost recovery rule applies to determine the amount of taxable income upon the surrender of a policy. Under that rule, the cost basis of the policy is deducted from the gross amount received to determine the taxable income. For this purpose, the policy owner's cost basis is normally comprised of the sum of premiums paid less dividends received. It should be noted that premiums for benefits such as waiver of premium and accidental death are not added to cost basis. In addition, if policy loans are outstanding upon surrender they will cause a reduction in cost basis. This presents a trap for the unwary where a policy with loans in excess of premiums paid is surrendered or allowed to lapse. The result is that the policy owner will have taxable income upon surrender or lapse of the contract, to the extent that the loans exceed the total premiums paid.

Modified Endowment Contracts "MECs". Pursuant to the Technical and Miscellaneous Revenue Act of 1988, policies meeting the definition of a Modified Endowment Contract or MEC receive a different tax treatment on pre-death distributions than other policies. This Congressional action was prompted by the practice of some companies selling single premium whole life policies more as tax deferred investment vehicles than as life insurance protection.

A MEC is defined by IRC Section 7702A as a contract entered into after June 21, 1988 that qualifies as life insurance under IRC section 7702 but fails to meet what is described as the 7-pay test. In that regard, a policy fails the test if the cumulative premiums paid at any time during the first seven years exceeds the sum of the net level premiums, which would have been paid on or before that time if the policy provided paid-up future benefits after the payment of seven level annual premiums.

The consequence of failing to meet the 7-pay test is that pre-death distributions are generally taxable to the extent of the "income on the contract". This means that such distributions are taxable to the extent that there is gain in the contract, on an income out first (LIFO) basis. (Pre-death distributions in excess of gain on the contract represent a nontaxable return of basis.) Further, policy loans or pledges against the contract are treated as distributions for this purpose.

Finally, distributions from a MEC are exposed to the 10% excise tax imposed by IRC Subsection 72(v).

Finally, it should be noted that the flexibility with respect to changes in face amounts and premiums, that is inherent with certain types of policies, subjects them to the risk of becoming a MEC.

Policy loans and interest. Except for MECs, as explained above, policy loan proceeds are not treated as taxable income. In addition, interest payments on such loans by individuals are not deductible. Under certain circumstances, however, interest payments by a business on loans against policies covering certain key persons are deductible within certain limits.

> **Some insurance policies permit death benefits to be paid if the insured is terminally ill.**

IRC Section 1035 policy exchanges. A life insurance policy may be exchanged for another life insurance policy or endowment or annuity contract without the recognition of taxable gain pursuant to IRC Section 1035. Under such circumstances the gain on the first contract is rolled into the second contract and the cost basis of the second contract is adjusted to include the basis of the first contract.

Accelerated death benefits. Some insurance policies permit death benefits to be paid if the insured is terminally ill. Generally, the proceeds will be income tax free under IRC Section 101(g)(1) if a physician certifies that the insured's medical condition can reasonably be expected to lead to death within 24 months. Similarly, proceeds received from a viatical settlement company on the sale of a policy are tax free under IRC Section 101(g)(2).

Note that a chronically ill individual may also receive income tax free proceeds but only if they are paid under a rider or other provision that is treated as a qualified long-term insurance contract under IRC Sections 101(g)(3) and 7702B.

Death proceeds. The general rule is that proceeds paid by reason of the death of the insured are exempt from income tax under IRC Section 101(a)(1). This includes the policy's face amount and any other insurance benefits that are paid because of the insured's death, such as accidental death benefits, term riders and paid-up additional insurance.

Death proceeds are, however, subject to taxation when the "transfer for value rule" is violated. This rule provides that if any interest in a life insurance policy is transferred for a valuable consideration, the death proceeds are taxable as ordinary income to the extent that the amount received exceeds the consideration and net premiums paid by the transferee. For example, assume Bill sells a $10,000 policy on his life to Susan for the policy's cash value of $3,000 and Susan subsequently pays $1,000 in net premiums before Bill dies. Upon Bill's death Susan will have a taxable gain of $6,000. This is calculated by deducting from the $10,000 of death proceeds the sum of the $3,000 consideration Susan paid Bill, plus the $1,000 of net premiums she paid to the insurer.

There are two classes of exceptions to the transfer for value rule that relate to (1) the nature of the transferee and (2) the nature of the transaction. With regard to transferees, an interest in a policy may be transferred to the following parties without violating the rule:

- the insured,
- a partner of the insured,

- a partnership in which the insured is a partner, or

- a corporation in which the insured is an officer or shareholder.

As to the nature of the transaction, the rule is not violated where the transfer does not result in a change in the policy's tax basis from the transferor to the transferee. The two cases when this occurs are transactions involving a bona fide gift from the transferor to the transferee, or a tax free corporate organization or reorganization.

Settlement options. Under settlement options, the death proceeds retain their income tax free status but earnings on those proceeds are taxable income. This means that under the interest option any interest is taxable. Similarly, under the installment and life income settlement options the payments are generally divided between taxable interest and a nontaxable return of principal.

Alternative minimum tax. Since 1986 corporations purchasing life insurance must consider the possible application of the alternative minimum tax. This does not necessarily mean that the ownership of the insurance will cause a minimum tax liability. Rather, the insurance cash values and death proceeds are only among many elements in determining whether the corporation will incur the liability. In addition, even when there is a liability, the effect is to tax cash value increases and death pro-

> If the corporation pays an alternative minimum tax liabilty in one year, that amount will be available as a credit against regular tax liability in future years in which there is no AMT.

ceeds at only a 15% rate. Further, the amount of the annual cash value increases may be reduced by the premium cost of the coverage, and death proceeds should be offset by cash value previously included in the calculation. Finally, if the corporation pays an AMT liability in one year, that amount will be available as a credit against regular tax liability in future years in which there is no AMT. Note that the Taxpayer Relief Act of 1997 exempts small corporations that meet a gross receipts test from the tax.

Federal estate tax. Death proceeds on the life of the insured are includable in the insured's gross estate, under IRC Section 2042, if the proceeds are payable to or for the benefit of the insured's estate or if the insured possessed incidents of ownership in the policy at death. Incidents of ownership include the right to name or change a beneficiary, take a policy loan, surrender the policy and other rights normally associated with policy ownership. It should be noted, however, that the insured does not have to own all the policy rights for the death proceeds to be included in his or her gross estate. Rather, the ownership of a single incident of ownership will cause the entire death proceeds to be included in the insured's gross estate. Further, if the insured gives away a policy or any incidents of ownership within three years of death, the death proceeds will be included in the insured's gross estate under IRC Section 2035. Finally, the value of policies owned by the insured at death on the lives of others will be included in the insured's gross estate under IRC Section 2033. Such policies are valued for estate tax purposes as they are for gift tax purposes substituting the date of death for the date of gift. (See gift tax valuation below.)

It is worth noting that characterization as life insurance causes the beneficiary of the death proceeds to have to reimburse the executor of the insured decedent's estate, under IRC Section 2206, for the federal estate tax that is attributable to the proceeds, unless provided otherwise in the insured decedent's will. On the other hand, because of such qualification under state law, life insurance is generally not subject to the claims of the insured's creditors as long as the death proceeds are not payable to the insured decedent's estate. (See PLRs 9119916 and 9146040.)

Federal gift tax. The gift of a life insurance policy is subject to federal gift tax. The value of the gift is based on the fair market value of the policy and is determined as follows:

- New policy: the gross premium paid by the donor to the insurer.

- Previously purchased paid-up or single premium policy: replacement cost, i.e., the single premium that the insurer would charge for the policy at the date of the gift.

- Premium paying policy: the interpolated terminal reserve. This is the policy reserve, adjusted to the date of the gift, plus the amount of any unearned premium.

Federal generation-skipping tax. The generation-skipping tax applies to transfers to skip persons that involve life insurance. For this purpose a "skip person" is defined as a person who belongs to a generation that is two or more generational levels below that of the transferor. In that regard, a generation-skipping transfer can involve the payment of

> **Avoid taxation on a substantial amount of life insurance through utilization of the donor's $1 million generation - skipping transfer exemption.**

death proceeds to a skip person through any means such as payment directly to the skip person or payment to a trust benefiting skip persons. Much can be done, however, to avoid taxation on a substantial amount of life insurance through utilization of the donor's $1 million GST exemption, as adjusted for inflation.

Chapter 6

Traps and Pitfalls to be Avoided

The purpose of this chapter is to provide guidance on how to avoid missteps in the following situations involving the use of life insurance. The list is not meant to be exhaustive but rather a reflection of more commonly made mistakes that can be prevented.

Multiple owner cases. When creating a joint interest in an insurance policy it is crucial to determine what the insurance company will do upon the death of a joint owner in regard to the ownership interests of the surviving joint owner(s). This depends upon the company's understanding of what the joint owners intended and what the company may presume in the absence of a clear understanding of their intention. To appreciate the implications of such a situation it is necessary to first review the differences between "tenants in common" and "joint tenants with right of survivorship".

Tenants in common share an undivided interest in an insurance policy and can leave their interest in the policy to another person at their death. For example, assume that X and Y own a policy on the life of Z, as tenants in common, and X dies. Upon X's death X's interest passes to whomever X designated in X's will or in the absence of a will the party designated by the state's intestacy law.

In contrast, joint tenants with right of survivorship share an undivided interest in a policy and if one of them dies, that person's interest automatically passes to the survivor(s). For example, if X and Y own a policy on Z, as joint tenants with right of survivorship and X dies, the policy becomes owned by Y.

> Joint tenants with right of suvivorship share an undivided interest in a policy and if one of them dies, that person's interest automatically passes to the survivors.

It is possible that, in the absence of a clear understanding of the parties' intention, the insurance company will presume which of the forms of joint ownership that they want in connection with a request for joint ownership. This means that the joint owners must be very careful that the insurer understands exactly whether they want tenants in common or joint tenants with right of survivorship. To avoid problems the request for joint ownership should clearly state "X and Y as tenants in common" or "X and Y as joint tenants with right of survivorship" and not just "X and Y" or "X and Y jointly".

In passing, it is worth noting that a gift of premiums directly to the insurer on a policy that is jointly owned will not qualify for the annual gift tax exclusion. That is because the joint owners' inability to independently access their shares of the gift will prevent the gift from qualifying as a gift of a present interest. To solve the problem have the donor write each joint owner a separate check for his share of the gift and let the joint owners subsequently write their checks for the premium to the company.

Third party owner not beneficiary. Whenever one person owns a life insurance policy on the life of another person the owner of the policy should also be the beneficiary of the policy, or he will make a transfer subject to the gift tax upon the insured's death. For example, if a mother owns a policy on the life of the father and names a child the beneficiary, upon the father's death, the mother will make a gift of the death proceeds to the child. (See Goodman v. Comm., 156 F2d 218 (2d Cir. 1946). Consequently, depending upon the circumstances, to the extent that the death proceeds exceed the mother's annual gift tax exclusion, they will reduce her gift tax applicable exclusion amount or generate a gift tax.

Trustee purchases of life insurance to avoid estate tax. A way for a prospective insured to avoid estate tax on the coverage is to establish an irrevocable Trust and provide the Trustee with funds to make the purchase. To avoid the risk of estate tax, if the insured dies within three years of the purchase, under IRC Section 2035, the policy should be acquired in a proscribed manner. In that regard, the Trustee, and not the insured, should be the applicant for the policy, and the Trust must be in existence when the application is submitted. It is not adequate that the application refer to a trust that is not in existence but is created a short time later. In such cases, the situation is likely to be treated as though the insured purchased the policy and then transferred it to the Trust. That would cause the death proceeds to be included in the insured's estate under IRC Section 2035 if he died within three years of his deemed transfer of the policy to the Trust.

Note that if a policy is to ultimately be owned by a Trust, it may be inadvisable to have it purchased by a family member who subsequently transfers it to a Trust. This is because the family member who acquires and transfers the policy will be making a gift to the beneficiaries of the Trust. Further, a portion of the policy's death proceeds will be included in the estate of the family member who buys and makes the transfer, if they are a beneficiary of the Trust and die before the Trust is distributed.

If the insured intends to acquire life insurance and wants to keep the death proceeds out of his estate through the use of a Trust, the best approach is to have the Trustee apply for the insurance and own the policy. That is because the three year rule of IRC Section 2035 will not apply if the Trustee makes the purchase and the insured dies within three years of that event.

To implement such a plan the proposed insured should establish a Trust and make gifts of cash to the Trust with which the Trustee can make the purchase. When making gifts to the Trust to finance premium payments, it is desirable to have such gifts qualify for the annual gift tax exclusion. That is because it allows the insured grantor to contribute $11,000 (as adjusted for inflation) to the Trust annually for each beneficiary gift tax-free ($22,000 per beneficiary if the insured grantor is married and the couple elects to split the gifts).

> **When making gifts to the trust to finance premium payments, it is desirable to have such gifts qualify for the annual gift tax exclusion.**

In order to qualify for the annual gift tax exclusion, however, the gifts must qualify as "gifts of present interest". That is deemed to happen automatically when the Trust is designed so that the death proceeds must be paid by the

Trustee to the beneficiaries on the insured's death. But that is not the usual design. If, however, the Trustee is required to retain the proceeds after the insured's death, gifts to the Trust will not qualify for the annual exclusion unless the Trust beneficiaries have been granted "Crummey withdrawal" rights as to the gifts.

The name Crummey comes from a court case in which it was decided that when a beneficiary has a right to withdraw gifts to the Trust, those gifts qualify as gifts of present interests. This approach operates by providing in the Trust instrument that when contributions are made to the Trust, the Trustee must notify the beneficiaries that each has a right to withdraw his share of the gift. Under the terms of such Trusts the power of withdrawal only exists for a limited period of time such as 30 days. That window of opportunity is sufficient, however, to make the gifts to the Trust, gifts of present interests that qualify for the annual gift tax exclusion.

Trustee for a minor beneficiary. It has been a long-standing practice of the insurance industry to permit a policy owner to designate someone as a "Trustee Beneficiary" for a minor when there is no Trust in existence. Nonetheless, the effectiveness of this practice depends upon state law, which may prohibit the designation from taking effect unless there is a Trust in place at the time the designation is made.

Oral trusts. Sometimes a prospective insured does not want to go through the expense and effort to create a written Trust to hold the policy. In that regard, while some states seem to allow the establishment of an

> **Oral trusts present practical problems because memories fade, and people change their minds.**

"oral trust" for personal property such as life insurance, the arrangement presents very practical problems and significant risks to the insurance company. That is because, with the passage of time memories fade, people change their minds while others die, and it becomes increasingly difficult to demonstrate the insured grantor's intention to create a Trust and/or prove its terms and conditions in the absence of a written trust instrument. Consequently, it is a far better practice to create a written Trust document or to utilize another form of transfer such as the Uniform Transfer to Minors Act.

Transfer for value rule. Any time an interest in a life insurance policy is transferred the transaction should be reviewed in light of the "transfer for value" rule of IRC Section 101(a)(2). This is because that rule can cause all or part of the policy's death proceeds to lose their income tax free status under IRC Section 101(a)(1). In that regard, the rule states that if any transfer of an interest in a life insurance policy is made for a valuable consideration, the death proceeds are subject to income tax to the extent they exceed the sum of the consideration paid plus premiums subsequently paid by the transferee.

There are two classes of exceptions to the transfer for value rule. The first includes transfers by gift to anyone and the second covers transfers to certain parties. Regarding the exception for certain parties the transfers covered are those to the insured, to a partner of the insured, to a partnership in which the insured is a partner or to a corporation in which the insured is an officer or shareholder.

• **Cross purchase buy/sell agreements.** Where a cross purchase buy/sell agreement is utilized the participants normally have to purchase multiple policies on each business owner's life. The actual formula for the number of policies required is N x (N-1) where N is the number of business owners participating in the agreement. For example, if there are five corporate shareholders, under a cross purchase agreement, the total number of policies they have to buy is 5 x (5-1) or 20 policies. As this is a burdensome approach to funding a buy/sell arrangement, it has been suggested that the participants need only establish a trust and have the Trustee purchase a single policy on each participant's life.

The problem with this approach is that it probably violates the transfer for value rule. That is because when a participant dies, that participants' interest in the policies on the surviving participants lives shifts to the survivors to fund future buy outs on the survivors' deaths. For example, if A, B and C have such an arrangement and A dies, his interest in the policy on B goes to C and his interest in the policy on C goes to B. Viewing these shifts of interests in light of the transfer for value rule, each shift may be a transfer for value with the consideration being the mutuality of each participant forgoing his interest in the coverage on the others at their deaths.

As previously stated, there is an exception to the transfer for value rule for transfers to a partner of the insured. Consequently, this exception allows a single-policy per participant approach to work where the participants to the cross purchase buy/sell agreement are partners in a partnership. In addition, it can work for the shareholders of a corporation if they are also partners in a separate partnership business.

• **Gift of a policy subject to a loan.** While there is an exception to the transfer for value rule for gifts of life insurance policies, it does not clearly apply to situations when the loan exceeds the donor's cost basis for the policy (for example, if the donor paid $15,000 of premiums on a policy with a cash value of $25,000 and a $20,000 outstanding loan). The reason is that the exception for gifts requires that the transferee's basis be determined in whole or part with reference to the transferor's basis. In that regard, Reg. 1.1015-4 that covers part gift/part sale transactions states that the transferee's basis is the greater of the transferor's basis or the amount paid, which would presumably be the amount of the loan. Consequently, using the above example, the transferee's basis would seem to be the amount of the $20,000 loan and not the transferor's basis of $15,000. This would mean that the transfer for value rule would seem to be violated, and the transferee's receipt of the death proceeds subject to income tax to the extent they exceeded the loan plus any premiums paid by the transferee.

It should also be noted that the transferor would have to recognize income on the gift to the extent that the loan exceeded the transferor's basis. ($20,000 loan - $15,000 premiums paid = $5,000.)

• **Starting or terminating split dollar arrangements.** Whenever setting up or terminating a split dollar life insurance arrangement, care must be taken that any shifts of interests in the policy fit into one of the above exceptions to the transfer for value rule. For example, if an existing policy is owned by a corporation and transferred to the insured to start an IRS Section 7872 type of interest free loan arrangement, there

> A transfer to the corporation by the insured to begin a split dollar endorsement arrangement would be exempt if the insured were an officer or shareholder of the corporation.

will be no problem since transfers to the insured are exempt from the rule. Similarly, a transfer to the corporation by the insured to begin a split dollar endorsement arrangement (governed by IRC Sections 61 and 83) would be exempt if the insured were an officer or shareholder of the corporation. Likewise, when the policy is formally transferred to the insured at termination of rollout of the endorsement arrangement, there is no problem since transfers to the insured are exempt. On the other hand, a transfer to a third party will not be exempt unless it is one of the exceptions, such as where the transferee is a partner of the insured.

Insurable interest and charitable gifts of life insurance. Some state's laws do not recognize that charities have an insurable interest in the lives of donors. Further, while most states have enacted legislation on the subject, the rules vary and can pose a trap for the unwary. For example, some states do not permit a charity to apply for and own a policy on a donor unless the donor consents to the purchase, while others do not permit a charity to make a purchase but allow an assignment of a policy to a charity.

The implications of not meeting a state's insurable interest requirement are that the insured's estate may be able to recover the death proceeds or premiums paid from the charity and there will be no income, gift or estate tax charitable deductions for the donor.

Glossary

Accelerated death benefit - A policy provision or policy rider that provides for the payment of all or a portion of the policy's face amount death benefit prior to the insured's death because of a terminal illness.

Accidental death benefit - A feature that provides for the payment of a multiple of the policy's face amount of death benefit in the case of the insured's death by accident.

Adjustable life insurance - A policy with a level premium and death benefit that gives the policy owner the ability, within limits, to modify the premiums, face amount and policy plan.

Alternative minimum tax - A tax imposed on corporations with gross receipts in excess of a certain amount that have substantial economic income but little or no regular tax liability.

Annual renewable term - A term policy with a level death benefit and an annually increasing premium.

Applicant - A party that applies for an insurance policy.

Beneficiary - A party that is designated to receive the death proceeds of a life insurance policy or for whom assets are held in a trust.

Buy term and invest the difference - An alternative to the purchase of cash value life insurance under which the purchaser buys term insurance and invests the difference between the term and equivalent cash value premiums in a mutual fund or other investment.

Cash value accumulation test - This is a test that cash value life insurance policies must meet to receive certain favorable Federal income tax treatment. Essentially, the cash surrender value of the policy may not at any time exceed the net single premium required to fund future policy benefits.

Cash value corridor test - A test which requires that a policy's death benefit be at least equal to certain percentage multiples of its cash value at all times in order for the policy to receive certain favorable Federal income tax treatment.

Cost basis - The amount of premiums paid less the amount of any dividends received which is used to determine the Federal income tax consequences of certain transactions involving a life insurance policy.

Cost of insurance - The charge each insured pays to cover his pro rata share of the death claims for a year.

Cross purchase buy/sell agreement - A contractual arrangement under which business owners agree to buy each others' interests during life or at death and fund their obligations with life insurance on each others' lives.

Current assumption whole life - A type of life insurance that has fixed premium and death benefit levels that may be changed periodically by the insurer to reflect new assumptions as to future earnings and mortality charges.

Death benefit - The amount paid by an insurance company upon the death of the insured.

Death proceeds - The death benefit plus any additional amounts paid under PUAs, term riders or as an accidental death benefit.

Dividend - The amount of distributable surplus paid to policyholders under a participating life insurance policy.

Donee - The person who receives a gift.

Donor - The person who makes a gift.

Executor - The party appointed in a decedent's will to administer his estate.

First-to-die insurance - A policy that pays a death benefit upon the first-to-die of two or more insureds covered under the same policy.

General account - The account an insurance company normally uses to hold assets that back its contractually guaranteed fixed payment obligations.

Gift - A transfer of property for less than adequate consideration.

Grace period - The period during which overdue premiums may be paid without the policy lapsing and without having to provide evidence of insurability.

Grantor - The person who creates a trust.

Guideline level premium test - A test for receiving certain favorable Federal income tax treatment under which the cumulative premiums for a policy must not at any time exceed the greater of the guideline single premiums or the sum of the guideline level premiums at that point.

Incontestable clause - A clause that prevents the insurer from voiding a policy for fraud, concealment or material misrepresentation after a certain period of time, that is usually two years.

Insurable interest - The expected financial gain or loss that a party has in connection with the continued life expectancy of a person and which serves as the legal basis for insuring the person's life under state law.

Insured - The person whose life is covered under a life insurance policy.

Insurer - A company issuing a life insurance policy.

Intestate person - A person who dies without a valid will.

Intestate succession statutes - State laws that dictate how the property of intestate persons' is distributed.

Joint tenancy with right of survivorship - A form of ownership by two or more persons by which the death of an owner causes that person's interest to automatically pass to the surviving owners.

Key person insurance - Life insurance that is purchased by a business to indemnify it from the financial losses associated with the death or disability of an important or key employee.

Limited payment cash value insurance - A policy that covers the insured's whole life but is paid up after a limited number of premiums.

Modified endowment contract - A life insurance policy that is issued after June 21, 1988 and meets the definitional requirements of IRC Section 7702 but fails the 7-pay test of IRC Section 7702A.

Net amount at risk - The difference between a policy's face amount and its reserve at a given point in time that is referred to as pure insurance protection.

Nonforfeiture provision - A provision that states how cash values may be applied upon termination of a policy.

Paid-up policy - A life insurance policy under which no further premiums are contractually required but which remains in force.

Participating policy - A life insurance policy that gives the owner the right to share in the company's surplus because actual experience is more favorable than assumed experience.

Planned premium - A premium amount selected by the policy owner and billed by the insurer under flexible premium contracts to avoid the risk of the policy lapsing for the nonpayment of premiums. It is sometimes also referred to a "target premium."

Policy illustration - A written description displaying guaranteed and non-guaranteed policy values over selected periods of time with other information that is intended to be useful to a prospective purchaser.

Policy owner - The party that holds the contractual rights and benefits to a life insurance policy in return for the obligation to pay premiums to the insurer. This party is also sometimes referred to as the "policyholder".

Premium - The specified amount that a policyholder is obligated to pay in return for the insurance policy.

Reinstatement clause - A provision that gives the policy owner the right to reinstate a policy after it has lapsed, such as by providing evidence of insurability and paying past due premiums.

Rider - The attachment to a life insurance policy that adds benefits such as term life insurance.

Second-to-die life insurance - A policy that covers two or more lives and pays a death benefit upon the death of the last to die. It is sometimes referred to as "survivorship" life insurance.

Separate account - An account that an insurer establishes apart from its general account to achieve results from a distinct group of investments.

Settlement options - The choices that a life insurance policy provides as to how the death proceeds will be paid.

Single premium cash value policy - This is a limited payment cash value policy that only requires the payment of one premium to make the policy paid-up.

Split dollar life insurance - An arrangement under which one party agrees to assist the other with the cost of a life insurance policy in return for the repayment of its funds from the cash value or death proceeds of the policy.

Surrender charge - A penalty that is paid to the insurer for the early termination of a life insurance policy.

Target premium - See planned premium.

Tenants in common - A form of joint ownership of property under which each joint owner may dispose of his or her undivided share of the property separately such as by will.

Transfer or value rule - A provision under IRC Section 101 by which all or a portion of the death proceeds of a life insurance policy may be subject to income tax.

Trust - An entity under which the Trustee holds legal title to property for the benefit of others.

Unbundled - A term used to describe a life insurance product for which the insurer separately discloses the pricing structure.

Uniform Transfer to Minors Act - State laws under which property is placed into the hands of a custodian for the benefit of a minor person until the minor reaches the age of majority. (Similar to the Uniform Gift to Minors Act.)

Variable life insurance - A type of cash value life insurance where the policy values vary directly with the results of a set of investments that are selected by the policy owner.

Variable universal life insurance - A type of cash value life insurance that combines the premium flexibility of universal life with the investment performance of variable life.

Waiver of premium - A feature under which the policy owner is not obligated to pay premiums if he or she becomes totally and permanently disabled before a certain age. In the case of current assumption and universal life coverages, the policy owner is relieved from the payment of mortality and expense charges.

Resource Guide

RECOMMENDED READING

New Life Insurance Investment Advisor
By Ben Baldwin

The most authoritative resource on today's most dynamic, versatile and adaptable investment vehicle. Term Life, Whole Life, Universal Life, Variable Life and more. Which products are best for you and your clients?? Discover the benefits of each for various client scenarios and life goals - and how to apply them when building solid client portfolios.
$29.95   Item #T182X-41593

Smarter Insurance Solutions
By Janet Bamford

A great handbook for financial professionals - or their clients - covering the skills needed to build and manage insurance "portfolios". Includes disability, health, life, personal liability, home, auto - and more.
$19.95   Item #T182X-5367

Insurance: From Underwriting to Derivatives
By Eric Briys & Franaois de Varenne

Over recent years, there has been great upheaval in the insurance industry. This book offers an in-depth look at the increasingly significant convergence between the insurance industry and the capital markets which has resulted in insurance being seen as an up and coming asset class.
$105.00   Item #T182X-17216

Protect Your 401(k)
By Larry Chambers & Ken Ziesenheim

10 Key Steps you MUST take to protect your - or your client's - retirement nest egg. More important than ever for advisors in today's post-Enron era, and loaded with specific, practical action items you can take to guide 401k's to both growth and capital preservation.
$10.95   Item #T182X-621482

The Long Term Care Planning Guide: Practical Steps for Making Difficult Decisions
By Don Korn

A compact new guide walks you through the maze of issues you need to consider when making long-term care choices. In his simple, straightforward style financial planning expert Don Korn focuses on the most common and crucial factors for determining long-term care needs.
$19.95   Item #T182X-820537

Dictionary of Insurance Terms
By Harvey Rubin

Lists thousands of specialized terms alphabetically with concise definitions, which should be understood by financial advisors, agents, brokers, actuaries, underwriters and other financial professionals and consumers. Newly updated edition reflect new technologies, their business applications, and recent business trends.
$14.70   Item #T182X-356399

Life and Health Insurance
By Kenneth Black & Skipper Harold

In this newly revised thirteenth edition, the authors continue their emphasis on combining current information about the life and health insurance industry's products and their uses with careful consideration of the environment.
$113.33   Item #T182X-12530

Understanding Erisa: A Compact Guide to the Landmark Act
By Ken Ziesenheim

This new guide clarifies the basic principles of ERISA - and the liabilities to which fiduciaries may be subjected - in simple, understandable terms. Perfect for establishing procedures within your practice, and for ensuring everyone in your organization is in compliance.
$19.95   Item #T182X-48535

Individually Managed Accounts
By Robert Jorgenson

Individually Managed Accounts: An Investor's Guide shows investors what IMAs are, how to use them, and the related pros and cons of investing in them compared to other investment alternatives. The first investor-friendly book on IMAs!
$59.95   Item #T182X-686489

Variable Universal Life

For advisors who need to explain this popular but complex insurance/investment vehicle to clients, this thorough guide and professional reference outlines all of the important considerations in detail. A Continuing Education product.
$29.00   Item #T182X-10951

The Complete Guide to Compensation Planning with Life Insurance
By Louis S. Shuntich, J.D., LL.M.

Help your clients attract and retain high caliber employees with this new, compact reference guide. The Society of Financial Service Professionals has teamed up with tax and compensation planning expert, Lou Shuntich, to bring it all together in one compact volume.
$29.95   Item #T182X-1611782

The Estate Planning Today Handbook
By Louis S. Shuntich, J.D., LL.M.

Learn to think like an estate planner so that you too can apply the step-by-step process of analysis that will enable you to identify your client's needs and match them to the appropriate solutions within your discipline.
$29.95   Item #T182X-1611781

IMPORTANT WEB SITES

www.insuranceplanningadvisors.com

Halloran Financial Services, specialists in estate and financial planning, providing comprehensive solutions for insurance and long-term care needs for over 20 years. For information contact:

> **Halloran Financial Services**
> Mike@insuranceplanningadvisors.com
> 781.449.4556
> 400 Hillside Ave, Needham, MA 02494

www.financialpro.org

For more than 70 years, the Society of Financial Service Professionals-formerly the American Society of CLU & ChFC-has been helping individuals, families, and businesses achieve financial security. Society members provide consumers expert assistance with: estate, retirement and financial planning; employee benefits; business and compensation planning; and life, health, disability, and long-term care insurance.

www.fpanet.org

The Financial Planning Association is the membership organization for the financial planning community. FPA's four Core Values - Competence, Integrity, Relationships and Stewardship - help to elevate and maintain the highest level of professionalism in the industry. FPA's primary goal is to advances the financial planning profession and the services it provides.

www.fpbooks.com

FP Books, a division of SuperBookDeals, is the #1 source for financial planning and investment books, videos, software, and other related products. Find the most thorough selection of new releases and hard to find titles geared towards financial planners and advisors.

www.iarfc.org

The IARFC is the fastest growing organization in financial services, increasing nearly 3% per month - now over 2,600 professional members. Prospects and clients expect that their financial advisors to maintain meaningful professional standards. There are seven hallmarks: education, examination, ethics, experience, licensing, continued conduct and continuing education. The RFC designation assures the public an advisor has, and will continue to maintain, the ability to serve in a professional, competent manner.

TRUST

It's a necessity,
not an indulgence,
in the investor-adviser
relationship.

Clients TRUST their
financial advisers to understand
the real goals that drive them.
But increased competition,
a continuously evolving industry
and unrelenting demands
are making it more difficult
to grow professionally and
guide your clients.

Society of
Financial Service Professionals®

Free 2 Week Trial Offer for U.S. Residents From Investor's Business Daily:

INVESTOR'S BUSINESS DAILY will provide you with the facts, figures, and objective news analysis you need to succeed.

Investor's Business Daily is formatted for a quick and concise read to help you make informed and profitable decisions.

To take advantage of this free 2 week trial offer,
e-mail us at customerservice@fpbooks.com
or visit our website at www.fpbooks.com where you
find other free offers as well.

You can also reach us by calling 1-800-511-5667
or fax us at 410-964-0027.

About The Author

Louis S. Shuntich served in the Law Department of a major life insurance company for 26 years where he specialized in business insurance and estate planning. He received his B.S. cum laude from Rider University, his J.D. from The College of William and Mary and his LL.M. (in Taxation) from New York University.

He is an associate editor of the *Journal of Financial Service Professionals,* a member of the Association for Advanced Life Underwriting Business Insurance and Estate Planning Committee, was chairman of the American Council of Life Insurance Split Dollar Task Force and has served on the Life Underwriter Training Council's Content and Techniques Committee. He is a member of the Speakers Bureau of the Society of Financial Service Professionals and the Speakers Bureau of the National Association of Estate Planners and Councils. He has also appeared on the CNBC Power Lunch and Health and Lifestyles programs answering questions about retirement and estate planning.

This book, along with other books, are available at discounts that make it realistic to provide them as gifts to your customers, clients, and staff. For more information on these long lasting, cost effective premiums, please call John Boyer at 800-272-2855 or email him at john@fpbooks.com.